What the Bible Says about Homosexuality:

A bible study for progressive people of faith

John Zehring

Copyright 2015 John Zehring

Table of Contents

Introduction

What the bible says
  about homosexuality

A study of the verses

The first two from
  the Leviticus Holiness Code

The third verse: Sodom

Paul's New Testament verses

The sixth verse: Romans

Interpretation

So what DOES the bible say?

Open and Affirming

What in the bible can I stand upon?

Stages of moral and spiritual development

How do I know what in the bible
  applies to me, if anything?

About the Author

Introduction

This work is based upon a sermon I gave as Senior Pastor at an Open and Affirming congregation of the United Church of Christ. Unlike most of my messages which were about twelve minutes long, this one was thirty-five minutes. That day I reduced every other part of the service so that I could offer a teaching message about the topic *What the Bible Says about Homosexuality*. My purpose was to teach about the topic but also to demonstrate what an in-depth study of the bible would look like. I took the tools of biblical exegesis and applied them to this message so that the texts would be considered within their historical, cultural and literary contexts. As always with a serious bible study, the first question to be studied is: *To whom was this passage addressed and to whom does it apply?* If a person were to get that part wrong, he or she could end up with a value system or worldview that is faulty because the biblical exegesis is faulty. So, it is critical for thinking people of faith to study and understand the context of a biblical passage.

Because much of the bible is based upon metaphor, symbolic language, cultural idiosyncrasies, and Middle Eastern teaching techniques, a reader of the bible must do the hard work of thinking, understanding and interpreting. Never is it sufficient for thinking people to say that they take the bible literally. The bible's writers never intended for each word in ancient languages to be taken literally as they are translated into modern English. They were wordsmiths, crafting their sentences to glorify God and to tell about God's mystery and majesty as best as humanly possible. In most cases, they had no idea they were writing Holy Scripture which would endure through the ages.

After my message about *What Does the Bible Say about Homosexuality*, a very intelligent and highly credentialed thinking person bolted out of church saying to nobody in particular, *"Well, then, what CAN I believe? How do I know what applies to me, if anything?"* That beautiful question led me to follow-up with another message related to the first, titled *What in the bible can I stand upon?* That is the second part of this work. It was a sincere question from a member who truly believed that the bible exists to tell about God's ways and explain how then we should live. If, he wondered, parts of the bible apply only to specific persons to whom they were addressed then and not to Americans in the 21st Century, how can he know what applies to him, if anything? A great question. Great questions always provide Pastors with opportunities for new messages.

If Jesus were standing in your presence right now, I think he would say *"You have to think. It is not all black and white. Use your mind."* And so, as you think about the topic and the bible's teaching, it is my prayer that the research and preparation I did for this work will help guide you, inspire you, inform you and lead you to glorify God in your extravagant welcome for all people, for each and every one has been pronounced good by the Creator.

A FEW NOTES ABOUT THIS BOOK

All scriptures in this work come from the New Revised Standard unless otherwise noted.

I have attempted to use inclusive language wherever possible in the words I have written, although I have not altered the author's reference to God as "he." I recognize that the Divine has no gender and for many it may be just as appropriate and accurate to acknowledge God as Mother or Father. Whichever pronoun we use, I consider God as a loving parent.

John Zehring

What the bible says about homosexuality

I would like to deal directly with what the Bible says about homosexuality, where I will try to give you the basic content of that the bible says about the topic. There is a lot to this topic and it can be divisive, so we want understand the biblical foundation upon which all else is built.

The topic can stir up emotions. Sound-bites, bumper stickers, placards, polarizing journalists and politicians and misquoting make us angry. We become so passionate that our thinking can become clouded and our behavior towards others has the potential to become unkind.

For this moment, let us take the time to be students, studying with an open mind the basic facts. Rather than proclaim a prophetic message here, I will wear the hat as a student of the bible to attempt, with intellectual integrity, to teach what the bible has to say about a topic. In some ways this is as much a lesson in how to approach the bible as it is about the topic.

If you Google *bible verses about homosexuality*, guess whose point-of-view dominates the websites? To double-check my research, I did that: I Googled. Seeing the unkindness and nastiness that raged out of some of these websites – many of them with a cross on their logo – made me ashamed to have them on my computer screen. It would be my guess that unkindness and nastiness like that makes God cringe. It was necessary to consult these websites, however, to make sure I left no stone unturned in discovering every biblical verse about homosexuality no matter how veiled or out-of-context was the reference.

There are 31,103 verses in the bible. After an exhaustive search, I have found six that pertain to homosexuality. There could be as many as eight. I might have missed one or two, but after double-checking my research with websites from fundamentalist, Christian right-wing and evangelical websites, I am pretty confident that half-a-dozen or so cover the territory. Of these six:

TWO are from the Old Testament book of **Leviticus** and say basically the same thing, so we might combine them.

TWO are from Paul's letters to the **Corinthians** and to **Timothy** which say almost the same identical thing. They are basically lists in which reference to *sodomy* is made, so we might combine these two.

ONE is from Paul's letter to **Romans** and

ONE is from **Genesis**, about the City of Sodom. This one has to be carefully studied to get the right message. Given what Ezekiel describes as the real sin of Sodom, I think we would be justified in excluding it from this study, but I will cover it.

So notice: there are **six verses** from **two men**: Moses wrote three and Paul wrote three.

There are six verses out of more than 31,000 on the topic. If you were to compare any topic by this measure, you would have to conclude that the bible does not seem to say much about that topic. Hence, the bible quantitatively says exceeding little about homosexuality. Be careful, however. There are critically important things in the bible that are mentioned once or twice. On the other hand, there are topics like sacrifices or dietary restrictions that are written about *ad infinitum ad nauseam*. The number of times a topic is mentioned does not necessarily give it more or less credibility.

There is a lesson here about the study of the bible and using the bible to guide your thinking, positions and actions which is: you need to look at the big picture. What is the overall message informing you about how to live in relation to God and to others? What is it, in your own personal life, behavior, thoughts and words that God expects of you? *What does the Lord require of you?* Real estate declares that its three most important characteristics are location, location, and location. The three most important characteristics of the bible's message are relationships, relationships, and relationships. The word *righteousness* in its best translation means *right relationships*. A key question in any detailed study of the bible is to ask how the text informs the believer about seeking to have the right relationship with God and the right relationship with God's children, which includes all women, men, girls and boys. No exceptions.

You can find some bible verse to support or contradict any position. It is easy to take words or verses out of context, so my message is: let us study this topic and every topic within the whole context of God's love and grace.

Should we emerge with differing points of interpretation after we have done our homework well and have been faithful to the text and the message of the bible, then let us agree that we as people of faith will not always agree about everything. Therefore let us extend kindness, love and grace to the other. Let us seek to build a community of faith where people are encouraged to think for themselves and where we may hold differing understandings and still be together as people of faith.

Now, consider a detailed look at the key six verses.

A study of the verses: The first two from the *Leviticus Holiness Code*

The FIRST TWO VERSES about homosexuality come from the Old Testament book of Leviticus, written about 1400 BC, more than 3,400 years ago. The authorship is ascribed to Moses who, according to Deuteronomy 34:7, lived to be 120 years old.

Leviticus 18:22 (NRSV):
You shall not lie with a male as with a woman; it is an abomination.

Leviticus 20:13 (NRSV):
If a man lies with a male as with a woman, both of them have committed an abomination; they shall be put to death; their blood is upon them.

You see how these two verses are similar. Both use the word *abomination*, although the second says that both should be put to death. That is the verse that people who have murdered gay people use to justify their crime as a holy act.

The first verse, *You shall not lie with a male as with a woman*, presumably is spoken only to men. Presumably these verses do not apply to women or to those who are bisexual or transgendered. Those last two categories are not covered at all in the bible.

Examine the first word: *YOU:* You shall not lie… Who does the *YOU* refer to?

When you study the bible, this is one of the very most important questions to ask: to whom is the verse spoken? To whom does it apply? Does the verse apply to everyone or just a specific person or group?

For example, consider this story from Mark 10:17-22:

As he was setting out on a journey, a man ran up and knelt before him, and asked him, "Good Teacher, what must I do to inherit eternal life?" Jesus said to him, "Why do you call me good? No one is good but God alone. You know the commandments: 'You shall not murder; You shall not commit adultery; You shall not steal; You shall not bear false witness; You shall not defraud; Honor your father and mother.'" He said to him, "Teacher, I have kept all these since my youth." Jesus, looking at him, loved him and said, "You lack one thing; go, sell what you own, and give the money to the poor, and you will have treasure in heaven; then come, follow me." When he heard this, he was shocked and went away grieving, for he had many possessions.

This is one of the greatest stories in the New Testament. Jesus is about to invite this man to become a disciple. It says Jesus, looking at him, loved him. That is a rare description, indicating that this is not an adversarial conversation in any way. Jesus would use the same words he spoke to his other disciples: *Come, follow me.* But the man could not accept the invitation because, as Jesus noted, *"You lack one thing; go, sell what you own, and give the money to the poor, and you will have treasure in heaven; then come, follow me."*

Here is how this connects to our study of the bible's text: *"You lack one thing"* was not addressed to you. It might apply to you or it might not. Perhaps there is something else that keeps you from following Jesus, in which case, you lack that thing. The overall message is that we must purge ourselves of anything that blocks us from loving God. But the specific message of the story from Mark 10 was spoken only to one man. Jesus did not require poverty as a condition for following him. He did not require the disciples to sell what they owned. *"You lack one thing"* was a specific prescription for a specific patient. It was not spoken to you and it does not necessarily apply to you, unless like the man in the story, your commitment to stuff prevents you from accepting Jesus' invitation to follow.

To return to the initial questions which must begin every serious study of the bible: to whom is the verse spoken? To whom does it apply? Does the verse apply to everyone or just a specific person or group?

If you will dig into bible commentaries, you will discover the Leviticus chapters 17-27 are known as *The Holiness Code*. The Holiness Code was directed specifically to the priestly cast of Israelites more than three thousand years ago. There are some Orthodox Jews today who try to live by this Holiness Code, but the Leviticus Holiness Code is not directed to or applicable to Christians in the 21st Century.

It was specifically for people who saw themselves as a kingdom of priests and as a holy nation (Exodus 19:6).

Jesus himself clashed with the Leviticus Holiness Code in the Gospel of John chapter 8 with the woman caught in the act of adultery. The law said she should be stoned to death. This code seems to have a fondness for stoning and killing, particularly for women. You notice that the man was nowhere to be seen.

As they picked up rocks to hurl, Jesus said *"Let anyone among you who is without sin be the first to throw a stone at her."* That could be applied to every one of us. And yet what Jesus said overrides and supersedes the Jewish Leviticus Holiness Code, written in the same section as these two verses about homosexuality. Jesus himself did not follow the Leviticus Holiness Code.

So why any Christian in 21st century America would think that you should follow the Leviticus Holiness Code when Jesus himself did not is a mystery and a misunderstanding.

The third verse about homosexuality from the story of Sodom

The THIRD of the six verses about homosexuality comes from Genesis chapters 13 through 19, which is about the City of Sodom. In the city were some who violated the Leviticus Holiness Code, men with men. This is where the term *sodomy* comes from: the city of Sodom. They would have been seen as an abomination, obviously, since the story of Sodom in Genesis was authored by the same man who wrote the Leviticus Holiness Code.

But I am going to make the case that we should not include these verses in what the bible says about homosexuality because, even though we really could lump them with the previous two, there is another reason which is Ezekiel's interpretation of what the whole story of Sodom and Gomorrah meant. In any passage or story from the bible, should not the serious reader desire to consider the overall meaning? Here is Ezekiel's bottom line, from Ezekiel 16:49: *This was the guilt of your sister Sodom: she and her daughters had pride, excess of food, and prosperous ease, but did not aid the poor and needy. They were haughty, and did abominable things before me; therefore I removed them when I saw it.* That was the sin of Sodom.

By this standard, we too would be an abomination before the Lord because, like the unrighteous people in the City of Sodom, we have had pride. We have been haughty.

Haughty means arrogant. Pride is a form of self-righteous, which may be the sin that Jesus and God hate most of all, as when someone thinks she or he is better than another, believing he or she is right and good while others are not. We are guilty of having more than enough food and prosperous ease, and yet how much aid do we really give the poor and needy? Look one more time at *the guilt of your sister Sodom*. The sin of Sodom, which is where the word *sodomy* comes from, is pride, self-righteousness, and not helping those in need.

So the message of Sodom in Genesis is not about sexuality but about lack of faithfulness to God and to how God's children are treated. Ironically, anyone who considers a homosexual person as inferior is committing the exact sin Ezekiel described. The one who looks down upon gay, lesbian, bisexual and transgendered persons is, by Ezekiel's description, committing sodomy.

Paul's New Testament verses about homosexuality

Now we move into the New Testament. Verses about homosexuality are not found in the gospels. Jesus spoke nothing about the topic. References to homosexuality exist exclusively in the letters of the Apostle Paul. The FOURTH and FIFTH verses about homosexuality are:

1 Corinthians 6:9-11 (NRSV):
Do you not know that wrongdoers will not inherit the kingdom of God? Do not be deceived! Fornicators, idolaters, adulterers, male prostitutes, sodomites, thieves, the greedy, drunkards, revilers, robbers – none of these will inherit the kingdom of God. And this is what some of you used to be. But you were washed, you were sanctified, you were justified in the name of the Lord Jesus Christ and in the Spirit of our God.

1 Timothy 1:9-11 (NRSV):
This means understanding that the law is laid down not for the innocent but for the lawless and disobedient, for the godless and sinful, for the unholy and profane, for those who kill their father or mother, for murderers, fornicators, sodomites, slave traders, liars, perjurers, and whatever else is contrary to the sound teaching that conforms to the glorious gospel of the blessed God, which he entrusted to me.

Both of these lists contain the word *Sodomites*, which is why the websites use these verses to make the case that homosexuality is a sin. Of course, there are a few other words in that list, like if you have ever had sexual intercourse with a person who is not your marriage partner or if you have ever taken anything that does not belong to you. It does not just say big things. So, if you make a photocopy of a copyrighted work without asking permission, you have taken something that does not belong to you. Idolaters? Is there anything you idolize more than God? The phrase *America's real religion* has been applied to sports, business, education, television, movie stars, shopping, and all kinds of things that people idolize. Perjurers? Ever tell a lie? Greedy… MOI! YOU? Did you ever have too much to drink… ever? We are on this list too.

Thank goodness that right after the list, Paul says God lets us off the hook. Paul adds *But you were washed, you were sanctified, you were justified in the name of the Lord Jesus Christ and in the Spirit of our God.* Thank God for the grace of God. Even people who judge *sodomy* a sin must accept that this verse about God's washing them clean applies to both the accused and the accuser.

Paul's two lists presumably define sin, along with an "other" category that includes whatever else is *contrary to the sound teaching.* It is in the bible. It says it clearly. Is it right? Does that mean that a person who is gay is a wrongdoer who will not inherit the kingdom of God?

We must be careful and diligent when applying Paul's message to specific members of a specific church in a specific culture two thousand years ago to our culture today. We cannot throw out the baby with the bathwater, but neither can we cling to his every word as applying to Christians in the 21st century.

In this very same letter to the Corinthians, Paul sees himself as speaking directly for God. He considers himself as God's mouthpiece, speaking as though what he said was neither debatable nor allowed to be questioned. Infallible. Direct divine revelation. But then, in the seventh chapter (vs. 12) Paul writes *"To the rest I say – I and not the Lord..."* This is Paul's announcement that he is now offering his own opinion. He is going *"off the record"* so to speak. It might be inspired, but he says it is only his personal point of view. What follows is not to be considered as divine revelation but rather the personal opinion of one man.

Perhaps Paul would have been well-served to have said this more frequently. There seem to be plenty of Paul's teachings which reflect his bias, his beliefs, his political persuasion, his opinion, his times and his culture. Would we think any less of the man had he just declared something to be his personal opinion rather than to insinuate that he was God's infallible mouthpiece?

Consider what church was like in Paul's day. There was no New Testament in print. The gospels were still being drafted. There were no creeds or statements of faith, no denominations, no judicatory staff and no church history. How could people considering these new beliefs measure them against some sort of orthodoxy to test their worthiness? Everything was unfolding and evolving.

Paul did not go to his word processor to write books of the bible or lasting literature. He was dictating letters to specific gatherings of people he had formed into churches. If you have ever tried to dictate a letter rather than to compose it by pen or by keyboard, perhaps you were surprised to notice how dictating letters has the potential to lead to long run-on sentences and wandering thoughts. Some of Paul's writings can sound that way. His letters might have been considered divinely inspired by his readers, but how could readers discern which was divine and which was personal observations?

Paul wrote in 1 Corinthians (7:25) *Now concerning virgins.* Oh boy, here it comes: Paul the authority on virgins. He wrote *I have no command of the Lord, but I give my opinion as one who by the Lord's mercy is trustworthy.* Okay. That is fair. Paul is giving his opinion. He even says this is not of the Lord: *I have no command of the Lord.* This is not up-to-the-minute live news from God. God is not speaking. This is Paul. He adds that he hopes is opinion is trustworthy but the opinion is his and therefore you can use it or not, accept it or reject it.

Speaking to a Greek, Roman or Asian culture two centuries ago, Paul wrote in his epistles things like:

*"**Slaves**, obey your earthly masters with fear and trembling, in singleness of heart..."* (Ephesians 6:5). This verse, along with three hundred other verses about slavery, was used as a cornerstone for defending the holding of slaves in America.

*"**Wives**, be subject to your husbands as you are to the Lord, for the husband is the head of the wife."* (Ephesians 5:22, 23). This verse has been used to justify all kinds of things, from domestic violence to preventing women from owning things.

Here is another from 1 Corinthians (14:35*): "If there is anything wives desire to know, let them ask their husbands at home. For it is shameful for **a woman to speak in church**."* This verse is used by some major denominations in America to prohibit women from being ordained as pastors or from even standing behind a pulpit.

Again in 1 Corinthians (7) Paul writes *"For the wife does not have authority over her **body**, but **her husband does**."* In that chapter Paul goes on to say get married if you must to avoid sexual immorality, but, he says, *"I wish that all were as I myself am.... To the unmarried and the widows I say that **it is well for them to**

remain unmarried *as I am. But if they are not practicing self-control, they should marry. For it is better to marry than to be aflame with passion."* Is that all that marriage means to Paul?

You get the picture? We must read Paul in the context of his times and his culture. Take from his writings what can be applied and helpful (for example, his stunning poem on love in I Corinthians 13) but we cannot and may not be selective to choose only verses that support our position but discount others which we do not favor.

In other words, if you take Paul's two verses with the word *sodomy* in them as applicable to Americans in the twenty-first century, you must also accept his verses about slavery, wives, virgins, women speaking in church, marriage (from one who was not married), and a bunch of sins, some of which may apply to you.

The sixth verse about homosexuality, from Paul to the Romans

The final of the six verses about homosexuality, from Paul to the Romans, is the verse that so polarizes our churches and our nation.

Romans 1:26-27 (NRSV):
For this reason God gave them up to degrading passions. Their women exchanged natural intercourse for unnatural, and in the same way also the men, giving up natural intercourse with women, were consumed with passion for one another. Men committed shameless acts with men and received in their own persons the due penalty for their error.

That is clear about what it says. Paul calls these acts unnatural and shameless. You can imagine what this verse has been used to justify.

If time allowed more of a detailed biblical exegesis of these verses, we could observe how Paul was specifically referring here to what he witnessed on his missionary tour of the Mediterranean where he saw great temples built to honor Aphrodite, Diana and other fertility gods and goddesses of sex and passion instead of the God which the apostle honors. The temple priests and priestesses engaged in some odd sexual behaviors which included castrating themselves, carrying on drunken sexual orgies and having sex with young temple prostitutes (male and female) – all to honor the gods of sex and pleasure. Paul is writing to the members of the new church in Rome about what he witnessed in Rome in these temples.

But return to the verse, because there is a logical inconsistency with it. Look at the first phrase: *For this reason God gave them up to degrading passions.* What Paul described as unnatural and shameless behavior was because God gave them up to what Paul called degrading passions. *For this reason.* For what reason? Here we have to trace our finger back in chapter one to verse 18 to find out who the *THEY* is to whom Paul is referring. *THEY*, wrote Paul, refers to those who refused to acknowledge and worship God, and for that reason were abandoned by God, which is very unlike the God Jesus taught about who does not abandon anyone. But this verse is not really about homosexuality. It is about faithfulness to God or about rejecting God.

There are countless homosexuals who have not rejected God at all. They love God. They acknowledge God as the one they follow, praise and worship. They thank God for God's grace and God's gifts. How, then, could they have been abandoned by God to homosexuality as a punishment for refusing to acknowledge God? They are indeed acknowledging God. This is a mountainous logical inconsistency.

Paul's opinion is that *THEY* gave up heterosexual passions for homosexual lusts. How can that be? They have been homosexual from the moment of their earliest sexual stirrings. They did not change from one orientation to another. They just discovered that they were homosexual. If anything is unnatural, it would be unnatural for most homosexuals to have heterosexual sex.

Gay and lesbian people do not lust after each other any more than heterosexual people lust after one another. Their love for one another is likely to be just as spiritual, personal and beautiful as any heterosexual love can be.

What Paul wrote to the Romans in chapter 1 is not about homosexuality today, but rather about Roman Temple prostitute practices in the first century and is no more applicable to 21st century Americans than Paul's views on women, marriage or slavery.

Interpretation

So, that is a look at the six verses. What can we say the bible tells us about homosexuality? Though the verses may not apply to us, these six say that in somebody's opinion and for somebody, homosexuality is an abomination, they should be put to death for it, they are wrongdoers who will not inherit the Kingdom of God and their behavior is degrading, unnatural and shameless. That leaves us with two choices: First, we either take these six verses literally (and therefore have a basis for a negative position on homosexuality), or, second, we recognize that the bible was never meant by the authors to be taken literally.

The writings are filled with metaphor, symbolic language, layers of meaning and Middle Eastern teaching techniques. Indeed, all language is symbolic and therefore subject to interpretation and understanding. So, our focus must be upon the love and grace of God. Therefore, we would conclude that the bible neither says nor means that there is anything wrong with homosexuality nor does the bible say it is unnatural or displeasing to God.

If a person were to claim to be a literalist, that is, if a person thought they could take the sixty-six books of the bible literally word-for-word, in modern English, then these six verses could substantiate a position that homosexuality is sin, it is wrong, it is unnatural and displeasing to God.

But wait: If that person is to be a literalist, he or she has got to take it all. A person cannot pick and choose what he or she will be literal about. A literalist cannot be selective about accepting what supports his or her views and rejecting those which do not. A literalist has got to take the whole shebang. For example, if you were to think that the Leviticus Holiness Code for orthodox Jews of 3,400 years ago applies to everybody today, then consider what else you must accept:

You would be required to **burn a bull on the altar** of your church that creates a pleasing odor for the Lord. Leviticus 1:9. Of course, your current altar might not hold the weight of a bull and your fire marshal may take a dim view of open fires inside public buildings.

You have full permission to **sell your daughter into slavery**, which is sanctioned by Exodus 21:7. However, if you do, you will break a civil law.

You are allowed to **own slaves**, but according to Leviticus 25:44 they must come from nations around you. That means people in the United States can own Mexicans or Canadians, but cannot own South Americans or Asians.

You are required to do **no work** on the SABBATH. The Sabbath runs from sundown Friday to sundown Saturday. If you do any work on the Sabbath, according to Exodus 35:2, you must be put to death. That includes multitasking!

You are not allowed to **cut your hair**, according to Leviticus 19:27. That is not a major problem for some of us who are folliclely challenged!

If it is discovered that a bride is **not a virgin**, Deuteronomy demands she be executed by stoning. It does not mention the groom's virginity.

Nobody who is **divorced** would want to take the bible literally, of course.

You may not touch the skin of a dead pig, says Leviticus 11:7, which means if you play **football**, you must wear gloves.

Sex with anyone who is **not your marriage partner**? Both are condemned to be stoned to death. It does not define who is authorized to carry out this death sentence.

There seems to be a fascination with killing those who violate all of these laws. Someone who holds to the Leviticus Holiness Code would obviously need to be an enthusiastic supporter of the death penalty. Society would need to build death rows in every town to handle all the violators. But is not all that killing in contradiction with God's commandment *"Thou shalt not kill"* or with Jesus' teachings about love, mercy, grace and forgiveness? If Christian love, *agape*, means to truly desire that which is in the other's highest and best interests, how could killing be in another's best interests? What about people out there who feel themselves authorized to judge your behavior, attitudes, words, values or beliefs? Do they not understand how clearly Jesus taught *"Judge not that ye be not judged?"* Who but God is good enough to judge another?

So what DOES the bible say about homosexuality?

So:
IF I could detach myself from the emotional and political hubris that divides people over this issue, and
IF I could look objectively as a student of the bible and parse the verses using the tools of biblical exegesis, and
IF I try to be fair and intellectually honest in my interpretation of God's word for humans today,
THEN I would have to say that the title of this work is incorrect because the bible does not say anything about homosexuality that can apply to us. My study of the bible leads me to the conclusion that the six verses usually quoted about the topic are not applicable to Christians in the 21st century.

What, therefore, does the bible say about how you should regard people who are gay, lesbian, bisexual and transgendered?

It says you should **love** them. *Agape* is the Greek word for love. The translation of *agape* is to want what is the other's highest interests, to truly desire what is best for them.

The bible says you should be **kind** to them. Unkindness is one of the worst sins. Unkindness is odious. It stinks. Gay people can be unkind too, but if you have been unkind or even nasty because a person is gay, you have sinned an ugly sin.

The bible says you should **do to them** as you would have them do to you, the Golden Rule. How would you desire to be treated?

The bible says you should give them **grace** and **forgive** them, just as they should give you grace and forgive you. Do not forgive them for being homosexual. Being homosexual is not a sin. Do not treat them as having a condition which stands in need of grace because of who they are. Grace is for people who have done something wrong. They may have done wrong like you and me, but being who they are is not one of those things.

The bible says you should **stop calling them *them***. *In Christ there is no East or West, in Him no South or North*, goes the hymn, *But one great fellowship of love, Throughout the whole wide earth*. That sounds pleasantly similar to Paul's letter to the Galatians 3:28: *There is no longer Jew or Greek, there is no longer slave or free, there is no longer male and female; for all of you are one in Christ Jesus*. It would be my guess that if the Apostle were here today, he would add *"there is no longer gay nor straight... for all of you are one in Christ Jesus."* So let us try to avoid the language of *us* and *them*. In Christ, we are one.

The bible says you should see them as **good**. The first verse of the bible declares that *In the beginning, God created the heavens and the earth*. God created, and everything God created God pronounced good. To consider anyone of God's creation as not good is to limit

God and to undermine God's creation. God does not make junk. God does not make mistakes. A person who has a disability is not a mistake. A person who is gay, lesbian, bisexual or transgendered is not a mistake. A person who is homosexual is God's beloved child, one who is created good and who is good. To consider any person not essentially good is to defy the Creator's handiwork.

I think what the bible says in most of those other 31,097 verses is we ought to get the message of what it means for you and me to be God-like: It is not God-like to judge another, to condemn another, to mistreat another, to deny rights to another or to be unkind. If we do that because someone is gay, lesbian, bisexual or transgendered, we are the ones in danger of being an abomination to our Creator.

Open and Affirming

I am proud to be a clergy member of an Open and Affirming denomination, the United Church of Christ. Actually, I have never liked the word "*affirming*," because I think that can be a misleading word.

Affirming does not mean to affirm another's lifestyle. It cannot mean that because anyone who thinks they have the power or authority to affirm a person's lifestyle must logically also think they have the power or authority to deny a person's lifestyle. The authority to affirm presumes the authority to deny. Your lifestyle is nobody's darned business. Another's lifestyle is not your darned business. Affirming or denying lifestyles is not the church's business. The church's business is to gather to worship God and scatter to serve God's children. The gathering of God's people is not in the business of affirming or denying lifestyles. If Christians started to affirm or deny lifestyles, where would it end?

I have come to see Open and Affirming as an island or a sanctuary where every person can come and not be judged for who they are. *Open* proclaims that we welcome all without exception. *Affirming* proclaims that we will not judge others but affirm that we will see each as a precious child of God, which, after the manner of the Golden Rule, is just how we would wish to be welcomed and seen.

I invited a gay man to come to church. He replied, *"John, I cannot go to your church. I am gay."* I quickly answered, *"But you are welcome. Didn't you see our sign? It says 'All are welcome!'"* He shot back, *"John, they all say that. But they don't mean me. I have walked to churches with that sign out front and later was told I would burn in hell unless I changed who I am. They do not mean All Are Welcome."*

God longs for the day when every community of faith will mean what they say on their sign and will extend an extravagant welcome to all without judgment, condemnation or unkindness. Then, when we open our arms widely in God-like fashion to welcome those who have not felt welcomed in many churches, those who are gay, lesbian, bisexual, or transgendered will feel the warmth of our extravagant welcome and know that we mean the Christian love we proclaim.

May God be glorified by our thoughts, our words, our deeds, and our extravagant welcome, especially to those who have felt unwelcomed in many places.

What in the bible can I stand upon?

TEXT: Matthew 7:12-14

MEDITATIONS:
He said to him, "'You shall love the Lord your God with all your heart, and with all your soul, and with all your mind.' This is the greatest and first commandment. And a second is like it: 'You shall love your neighbor as yourself.' On these two commandments hang all the law and the prophets." (Matthew 22:37-40 NRSV)

Then Peter came and said to him, "Lord, if another member of the church sins against me, how often should I forgive? As many as seven times?" Jesus said to him, "Not seven times, but, I tell you, seventy-seven times. (Matthew 18:21, 22 NRSV)

Do to others as you would have them do to you. (Luke 6:31)

After the message *What does the bible say about homosexuality?"* a member rushing out of church was overheard to say to nobody in particular, *"Well, then, what CAN I believe? How do I know what applies to me, if anything?"* His question reflects the sincere wonderings of many people of faith as they contemplate what foundation they can stand upon. Where is the rock-solid place to stand upon which other beliefs can build?

There was a philosopher named Archimedes, born in Syracuse, Sicily. He was also a mathematician and inventor. He invented the lever. Before Archimedes, no one could lift very much but after him a person could lift a piano, a car or even a building. Archimedes could lift anything, he said, as long as he had a fulcrum, a fixed place to stand and a bar. He would put the weight on the short end of the bar and he would operate the long end of the bar and he would seem to be able to lift anything.

The King of Syracuse asked the question, *"Archimedes, how much can you lift?"*

Archimedes answered *"If you give me a place to stand, I can lift the whole world."*

People of faith long for fixed places to stand, for some absolutes. What in the bible can you stand upon? What do you know for certain is the absolute truth, something you can hold on to, cling to, trust in, count on and use as a rock-solid foundation to base your beliefs upon? Where can you put your foot down and stand upon solid ground?

A bumper sticker read *God said it, I believe it, That settles it.* It might be nice if it were that simple, but the bumper sticker actually sounds simplistic and anti-intellectual, for God gave us minds and expects us to use them. We must base our beliefs on an informed faith, on correct interpretations of scripture and on realizing that not everything is so black and white.

When I was a child,
I spoke like a child,
I thought like a child,
I reasoned like a child;
When I became an adult, I gave up childish
ways. (from I Corinthians 13)

There is a difference between being child-like and childish.

Stages of moral and spiritual development

Harvard psychologist Lawrence Kohlberg said that a person's moral development evolves, moving through stages. In the infant stage, everything is seen in terms of black and white. The rules are fixed and absolute. No exceptions. Mother tells child to do something, child dutifully obeys. Child cannot change the rules. Life is a balance of law and order.

As children grow, they begin to test the rules and to see that there are shades of gray. The older child's view becomes more relativistic. He or she understands that it is permissible to change rules if everyone agrees. Rules are not sacred and absolute but are devices which humans use to get along cooperatively. Moral choices are not always clear. As humans mature, they develop increased capability to consider others rather than their own self-interest, to realize there are consequences of behavior and even to see the greater good.

Humans progress and grow through stages of moral development, said Kohlberg, from the black and white absolutes to the highest level of choosing not only that which makes for a society that functions well but for making moral choices because they are good, right and just.

But not everyone grows at the same pace. Some, Kohlberg said, get stuck. There can be adults who get stuck at level one or two, where they require the world to be seen in black and white. Some get stuck at levels four or five. Lower levels require one only to follow the black and white absolutes. As humans mature, they realize that moral development must be interpreted. *When I became an adult, I gave up childish ways.*

Is it not the same with spiritual development? There is growth from following and obeying black and white absolutes to needing to reflect, analyze, evaluate, interpret and understand. An unthinking faith is a dangerous faith. An uncritical faith could lead to making up your own do-it-yourself religion and believing whatever reinforces your own world-view. A person could be way off-base. An uncritical faith could allow acceptance of the word from the pulpit, radio or TV as though it were accurate, authoritative, correct or even infallible, especially if proffered by a winsome personality.

Unethical charismatic leaders cherish nothing better than those who follow with a blind emotional faith, for how easily they can be manipulated and swept away into a cult of personality. Wishy-washy sentimentality thrives in the pulpit where members favor a Hallmark card theology that does not challenge them to wrestle with complicated and sometimes conflicting ideas.

How do I know what in the bible applies to me, if anything?

That is the key question. Short answer: In every case, you have to think. You must study, learn, educate yourself and use your mind to interpret the bible for your times. An unthinking faith is a dangerous faith. It can never be sufficient to hold that *"God said it, That settles it, I believe it."*

To be intellectually honest and to interpret God's word with integrity requires the believer to evaluate that not everything spoken in the bible was said to you or applies directly to you. You might be inspired or challenged by a text, you might base your faith and hope upon it, you might see how the basic principle applies to you, but God did not necessarily address it to you.

As I consider my years of studying the bible, here is how I would answer the question for myself: *What in the bible can I stand upon?*

I can stand upon Jesus' TWO GREAT COMMANDMENTS: *"'You shall love the Lord your God with all your heart, and with all your soul, and with all your mind.' This is the greatest and first commandment. And a second is like it: 'You shall love your neighbor as yourself.' On these two commandments hang all the law and the prophets."* (Mat 22:37-40).

Did you catch that last part? *On these two hang all the law and the prophets.* Everything: The Ten Commandments, the hundreds of interpretations, the Leviticus Holiness Code, all the other rules, rights and wrongs, do's and don'ts hang on these two. All the law and the prophets hang on right relationships. You are required to interpret and to question: Who is my neighbor? Jesus had to explain that, as he answered with the parable of the Good Samaritan. What does it mean to love and how far do I take this? Are there limits? What about my enemies? From the Mount, Jesus offered what is considered the most Christian verse in the New Testament: *Love your enemies.*

I can stand upon the SERMON ON THE MOUNT in Matthew 5, 6 and 7. There are parts hard to understand and some teachings which applied specifically to Jesus' particular audience, the twelve disciples, but overall, the Sermon on the Mount is a substantial building block of faith, albeit one that needs understanding, reflecting and interpreting.

I can stand on Jesus' teaching about FORGIVENESS. How often, seven times? No, said Jesus to Peter, seventy times seven, which was his metaphoric way of saying there are no limits to forgiveness. God's forgiveness is limitless and if we desire to be God-like, we too will not limit our forgiveness.

I can stand upon THE GOLDEN RULE. This is the Mount Everest of human ethics and moral development. Here it is, from Luke 6 (31): *Do to others as you would have them do to you.* Those are eleven of the most important words ever cobbled together in the history of human civilization. Ten of them are only one syllable. All the words are common and simple. In combination, they form the highest ethical teaching of humankind.

The Golden Rule by itself is not enough. It is good, but it is not the same thing as being a person of faith. It must be coupled with the commandment to LOVE GOD and LOVE NEIGHBOR. Loving neighbor alone is not enough. The highest commandment in the bible is: *You shall love the Lord your God with all your heart, and with all your soul, and with all your mind.* (Matt 22:37)

How can metaphors apply to me?

Oh, Archimedes: where is the place I can stand with sure footing?

All language is symbolic. All words are symbols. Many of the bible's teachings are metaphors. Does that mean that they are not true? Oh no. *"For Thou are with me, thy rod and thy staff, they comfort me."* The rod and the staff are metaphors. They deeply symbolize God's care and protection. And yet, the comfort is very real and true. This metaphor has comforted generations over the centuries in their valley of the shadow of death.

Many of the bible's teachings were spoken to a specific person, not to you. Does that mean they do not apply to you? Consider again the bible's wonderful example of the rich young ruler who came to Jesus and Jesus was about to invite him to become a disciple. They discussed the commandments. In earnest sincerity, the young man affirmed that he had kept all these rules since his youth. Whatever was in black and white, he kept them literally. Think level #1 of Kohlberg's stages of moral development. Jesus looked at him and said *"There is one thing you lack. Go, sell what you have and give it to the poor, and come, follow me."*

Jesus spoke those words specifically to that young man, not to you. Jesus never required poverty as a prerequisite for discipleship. Jesus did not tell you to sell all that you have. The message may apply to you. You may lack one thing that holds you back from you following him with all your heart. It might be money or stuff. It might be something else, another need or want. Even though the words spoken here may not apply to you, the message applies in a very profound way: what do you lack that is holding you back? If you want to follow Jesus completely, you must get rid of it. This is extreme Christianity. Jesus expects people of faith to do no less than to place God first in their lives.

In the novel *The DaVinci Code* by Dan Brown, at the very end of the quest for the Holy Grail, which was not what they thought it was, Robert Langdon says to Sophie Neveu: *"The problems arise when we begin to believe literally in our own metaphors."* Even Archimedes' reply to the King of Syracuse was a metaphor: *"If you give me a place to stand, I can lift the whole world."* That is true and the lever would work, but there is no literal place to stand and no lever that long.

What in the bible can you stand upon?

I have provided a list of the great mountains of the bible that I believe I can stand upon. All of the rest has value to our understanding of God's ways, although it requires reflection, understanding, analysis, evaluation and interpretation. We must think. We must use the minds God gave us.

And yet, here is the paradox: When it comes to faith, it is the simple childlike trust, love and obedience that pleases God most. Jesus said: *Truly I tell you, unless you change and become like children, you will never enter the kingdom of heaven.* (Matthew 18:3 NRSV)

Even that is a metaphor, but isn't that just like God to make it that clear and simple?

#

About the Author

John Zehring has served United Church of Christ congregations for twenty-two years as Senior Pastor in Massachusetts (Andover), Rhode Island (Kingston), and Maine (Augusta) and as an Interim Pastor (Arlington, MA). Prior to parish ministry, he served in higher education for more than two decades, primarily in development and institutional advancement, as a dean of students, director of career planning and placement, professor of public speaking and as a vice president at a seminary and at a college.

He is the author of more than two dozen books and eBooks. His most recent book, planned for release by Judson Press in May 2016 is *Beyond Stewardship: A Church Guide to Generous Giving Campaigns*. Previous print books include *You Can Run a Capital Campaign* (Abingdon Press), *Working Smart: a Guide for New Managers* (Garrett Park Press), *Careers in State and Local Government* (Garrett Park Press), *Making Your Life Count* (Judson Press), and *Preparing for Work* (Victor Books). His articles have also been published in more than 200 magazines and journals.

Recent eBooks, available from eBook retailers, include
Clergy Guide to Sermon Preparation: Including 40 Sermon Ideas and Outlines
Mount Up with Wings: Renew Your Strength
Jesus' Sermon on the Mount: Matthew 5, 6 and 7
Psalm 23: An Everyday Psalm
Seven Mantras to Shape Your Day: Bible Verses to Improve How You See Things
The One Minute Beatitude: A Brief Review of Jesus' Beatitudes.

Treasures from Philippi: GEMS for You from the Epistle to the Philippians.
To Know God Better and *To Love God More: Messages* for *Your Spiritual Journey.*
Did He Hit Her? A Compassionate Christian Response to Abusive Relationships
What the Bible Says About Homosexuality: A Bible Study for Progressive People of Faith.
For People of Faith, Torture is Always Wrong
Public Speaking for Executives, Leaders & Managers
Visiting on Behalf of Your Church: A Guide for Deacons, Care Teams and Those Who Visit
Clergy Guide to Making Visits
Clergy Public Speaking Guide: Improve What You Already Do Well.
Clergy Negotiating Guide: Don't Sell Yourself Short.

John served as a consultant, a keynote speaker, a workshop leader, a professor at the college and seminary level, and a director on boards of directors for UCC Conferences in Massachusetts, Rhode Island and Maine. He has taught Public Speaking, Creative Writing, Educational Psychology, and Church Administration. He was the founding editor of the publication *Seminary Development News*, a publication for seminary presidents, vice presidents and trustees (published by the Association of Theological Schools, funded by a grant from Lilly Endowment). He graduated from Eastern University and holds graduate degrees from Princeton Theological Seminary, Rider University, and the Earlham School of Religion.

John is married to his high school sweetheart Donna and they have two children and five grandchildren. He lives in two places, in central Massachusetts and by the sea in Maine where he and Donna enjoy kayaking, skiing, snowshoeing, gardening, using favorite tools, taking rides, travel and most of all being with family, friends and neighbors.

Made in the USA
Las Vegas, NV
27 November 2020